# Sirens

by Deborah Zoe Laufer

A Samuel French Acting Edition

New York Hollywood London Toronto

SAMUELFRENCH.COM

Copyright © 2011 by Deborah Zoe Laufer

ALL RIGHTS RESERVED

Cover photo by Harlan Taylor,
Copyright © by Actors Theatre of Louisville
Actress pictured: Lindsey Wochley

CAUTION: Professionals and amateurs are hereby warned that *SIRENS* is subject to a licensing fee. It is fully protected under the copyright laws of the United States of America, the British Commonwealth, including Canada, and all other countries of the Copyright Union. All rights, including professional, amateur, motion picture, recitation, lecturing, public reading, radio broadcasting, television and the rights of translation into foreign languages are strictly reserved. In its present form the play is dedicated to the reading public only.

The amateur and professional live stage performance rights to *SIRENS* are controlled exclusively by Samuel French, Inc., and licensing arrangements and performance licenses must be secured well in advance of presentation. PLEASE NOTE that amateur licensing fees are set upon application in accordance with your producing circumstances. When applying for a licensing quotation and a performance license please give us the number of performances intended, dates of production, your seating capacity and admission fee. Licensing fees are payable one week before the opening performance of the play to Samuel French, Inc., at 45 W. 25th Street, New York, NY 10010.

Licensing fee of the required amount must be paid whether the play is presented for charity or gain and whether or not admission is charged.

Professional/stock licensing fees quoted upon application to Samuel French, Inc.

For all other rights than those stipulated above, apply to: William Morris Endeavor Entertainment, LLC 1325 Avenue of the Americas, New York, NY 10019; attn: Derek Zasky.

Particular emphasis is laid on the question of amateur or professional readings, permission and terms for which must be secured in writing from Samuel French, Inc.

Copying from this book in whole or in part is strictly forbidden by law, and the right of performance is not transferable.

Whenever the play is produced the following notice must appear on all programs, printing and advertising for the play: "Produced by special arrangement with Samuel French, Inc."

Due authorship credit must be given on all programs, printing and advertising for the play.

**ISBN 978-0-573-69929-0**   Printed in U.S.A.   #29713

No one shall commit or authorize any act or omission by which the copyright of, or the right to copyright, this play may be impaired.

No one shall make any changes in this play for the purpose of production.

Publication of this play does not imply availability for performance. Both amateurs and professionals considering a production are strongly advised in their own interests to apply to Samuel French, Inc., for written permission before starting rehearsals, advertising, or booking a theatre.

No part of this book may be reproduced, stored in a retrieval system, or transmitted in any form, by any means, now known or yet to be invented, including mechanical, electronic, photocopying, recording, videotaping, or otherwise, without the prior written permission of the publisher.

## MUSIC USE NOTE

Licensees are solely responsible for obtaining formal written permission from copyright owners to use copyrighted music in the performance of this play and are strongly cautioned to do so. If no such permission is obtained by the licensee, then the licensee must use only original music that the licensee owns and controls. Licensees are solely responsible and liable for all music clearances and shall indemnify the copyright owners of the play and their licensing agent, Samuel French, Inc., against any costs, expenses, losses and liabilities arising from the use of music by licensees.

## IMPORTANT BILLING AND CREDIT REQUIREMENTS

All producers of *SIRENS* must give credit to the Author of the Play in all programs distributed in connection with performances of the Play, and in all instances in which the title of the Play appears for the purposes of advertising, publicizing or otherwise exploiting the Play and/or a production. The name of the Author *must* appear on a separate line on which no other name appears, immediately following the title and *must* appear in size of type not less than fifty percent of the size of the title type.

In addition the following credit *must* be given in all programs and publicity information distributed in association with this piece:

**World Premiere in the 2010 Humana Festival of New American Plays At Actors Theatre of Louisville**

**actors** theatre of louisville

**34th annual Humana Festival of New American Plays**
made possible by a generous grant from The Humana Foundation

# Sirens

by **Deborah Zoe Laufer**
directed by **Casey Stangl**

### THE CAST
(in order of appearance)

| | |
|---:|:---|
| Sam Abrams | **Brian Russell**\* |
| Rose Adelle Abrams | **Mimi Lieber**\* |
| Leah/Siren/Waitress | **Lindsey Wochley**\* |
| Richard Miller | **Ben Hollandsworth**\* |

*Various locations in Manhattan and the Mediterranean Sea.*

Presented by arrangement with William Morris Endeavor Entertainment.

| | |
|---:|:---|
| Scenic Designer | **Michael B. Raiford**† |
| Costume Designer | **Sonya Berlovitz**† |
| Lighting Designer | **Jeff Nellis**† |
| Sound Designer/Composer | **Matt Callahan** |
| Properties Designer | **Mark Walston** |
| Wig/Makeup Designer | **Heather Fleming** |
| Stage Manager | **Stephen Horton**\* |
| Dramaturg | **Julie Felise Dubiner** |
| Casting | **Emily Ruddock, Zan Sawyer-Dailey** |

Developed at Geva Theatre Center, Rochester, N.Y.
and Florida Stage's 1st Stage New Works Festival, Manalapan, Fla.

\*Member of Actors' Equity Association, the union of professional actors and stage managers of the United States
†Designers that are represented by United Scenic Artists, Local USA 829 of the IATSE

## CHARACTERS

**SAM ABRAMS** – 40s-50s
**ROSE ADELLE ABRAMS** – 40s-50s, Sam's wife
**SIREN** – Sublimely lovely. Early 20s. (Also plays: **LEAH**, **WAITRESS**)
**RICHARD MILLER** – 40s-50s; Played by an actor in his early 20's

## A NOTE ON THE MUSIC

For rights to the music from the original Actors Theatre of Louisville Humana production, please contact composer Matt Callahan at CallahanMatthew@hotmail.com for more information.

*(At the top of the play, as the audience is settling, we should hear three different versions of Sam's song, "Rose Adelle." And then, with each scene break we should hear another version. Perhaps Billy Joel. Mel Torme. A Japanese version. A cell phone ring tone. Musak. Captain and Tenille. The song is ubiquitous.* **SAM** *can't escape it.)*

**ROSE ADELLE.**
> ROSE ADELLE, ROSE ADELLE
> LOOKED MY WAY AND HOW I FELL
> BUT JUST ONE KISS FROM YOUR SWEET LIPS AND HOW I
>    ROSE ROSE ROSE
> ROSE ADELLE
>
> COME DOWN COME DOWN COME DOWN TO ME BABY
> COME DOWN COME DOWN COME DOWN TO ME BABY
>
> COME DOWN FROM YOUR SWEET PINK BEDROOM
> DRIVE DOWN TO THE LAKE WITH ME
> DOWN WHERE YOUR PARENTS CAN'T SEE US BABY
> WE'LL UNCOVER SOME MYSTERY
> I'M BURNING UP WHEN I THINK OF YOU BABY
> IT'S DRIVING ME INSANE.
> COME TO THE LAKE TO COOL MY FIRE
> OR SET US BOTH AFLAME.
>
> ROSE ADELLE, ROSE ADELLE
>
> LOOKED MY WAY AND HOW I FELL
> BUT JUST ONE KISS FROM YOUR SWEET LIPS AND HOW I
>    ROSE ROSE ROSE
> ROSE ADELLE

## Scene One

*(**SAM** and **ROSE ADELLE** are at a travel agency. The backdrop is saturated with bright island scenes, while they seem small and gray. **ROSE** is constantly knitting. It is a long train, narrower than a scarf, so long that it winds around and around her.)*

*(Note: **SAM** and **ROSE** speak over each other in the way long-married couples might. The /'s reflect when the next character begins speaking.)*

**SAM.** What if Barry decides to come home?

**ROSE.** I told you, he's going to Courtney's house. Her parents.

**SAM.** But what if he changes his mind? And then we're away.

**ROSE.** You're hilarious. We should just wait home by the phone for the next thirty years? I told you she makes the decisions/ now.

**SAM.** It's nice that he's got a girl, hon. When we were in college, remember how great it was /when we…

**ROSE.** All those years of late nights and fevers and term papers and bullies and all the things we worried ourselves sick over. Now "Courtney" decides where he goes.

*(During this, **LEAH** walks past, perhaps pausing to look through some papers. She is tall and willowy and lovely. There is a faint wisp of music heard. Maybe a harp. **SAM** is transfixed by the sight of her. He is quietly humming to himself, trying to remember…Everything else disappears.)*

I said, "Didn't you go to Courtney's parents' for Winter break? Don't you think it would be nice to come see your parents this time, let us get to know her?" "Maybe next break," he says.

**LEAH.** *(on her way out)* I'll be with you folks in just a moment!

*(**SAM** watches her leave, still humming, hungrily, longingly.)*

**ROSE.** Sam. *(pause)* Sam!

**SAM.** Right! So…

**ROSE.** Am I here?

**SAM.** Huh?

**ROSE.** Do you see me here? Do you hear me when I talk?

**SAM.** …So maybe he'll come next break!

**ROSE.** Sure.

**SAM.** She sounds nice. On the phone.

**ROSE.** How is she going to sound? She's going to say, "Hello Barry's father – piss off"?

**SAM.** *(looking around self-consciously)* Rose…shhhh.

**ROSE.** He'll see. He likes the soft part of the bread, so I ate the crusts. You think she'll eat the crusts?

**SAM.** They can throw away the crusts.

**ROSE.** You think she'll get him a cup of water in the middle of the night? Rub his cheek when he has a bad dream?

**SAM.** That was when he was four, /hon.

**ROSE.** He'll wake up from his bad dream and we'll be on vacation.

**SAM.** Yeah. Then, maybe we shouldn't /go.

**ROSE.** It's fine. It'll be fine.

**SAM.** Why don't we just drive to the Jersey shore again? Remember?

**ROSE.** That's hilarious.

**SAM.** When we did that?

**ROSE.** I did not put up with you for twenty-five years to go to the Jersey/ Shore.

**SAM.** Maybe Maine? Or D.C. We could drive to D.C.

**ROSE.** I'm taking three weeks vacation. Peggy's covering/ for me.

**SAM.** Three weeks? Oh my God.

**ROSE.** We're going…far. We're doing something special.

*(LEAH reenters. Maybe a harp is heard again.)*

**LEAH.** Hi. I'm Leah Peters.

**ROSE.** Hello.

**SAM.** Leah Peters.

**LEAH.** What can I help you with today?

**SAM.** What a beautiful name.

**LEAH.** You looking for a vacation package?

**SAM.** You look like you should be in high school.

**ROSE.** *(sighs, annoyed)* Sam.

**LEAH.** I assure you, Sir. I'm a qualified travel agent.

**ROSE.** He didn't mean that, Sweetheart.

**LEAH.** I've been working professionally for several months.

**ROSE.** He's flirting with you. Just ignore him. We're looking for something special. For our twenty-fifth wedding anniversary.

**LEAH.** Twenty-five years! Wow.

**ROSE.** You're telling me.

**LEAH.** That's quite an accomplishment.

**ROSE.** You have no idea.

*(Both women laugh at this.)*

**LEAH.** I have a fantastic cruise package to the Mediterranean that might interest you. It's really special.

**ROSE.** We want something special.

**LEAH.** *(reading off her clipboard)* Let's see…explore the Greek Isles. Chart the journey of Odysseus.

**SAM.** A cruise?

**LEAH.** I just got this in. You're the first clients I'm offering this to.

**SAM.** Aren't there stories…about/ cruises…

**ROSE.** Nothing. There's nothing. It's fine.

**SAM.** There was an article. About these cruise ships. Disappearing.

*(There is a pause and then both women burst out laughing.)*

**ROSE.** Disappearing?! Like…Brigadoon?

**LEAH.** You're so cute! He's so cute.

**ROSE.** He's hilarious.

**SAM.** There were stories. Recently. Online.

**ROSE.** No, that sounds perfect. The Greek Isles.

**LEAH.** Ok. So! Let me get some of your information, and then I'll find those brochures. And we'll just agree that you're mine, I mean, my clients, so if you come back in you just ask for Leah Peters, okay?

**SAM.** Absolutely.

**LEAH.** Here's my card.

*(**SAM** reaches for it. **ROSE** grabs it first.)*

Ok! So…your names are…

**SAM.** Sam and Rose Abrams.

**ROSE.** Rose Adelle.

**LEAH.** Oh! Like the song.

**ROSE.** Exactly like the song.

**SAM.** Honey…

*(He sighs, embarrassed already.)*

**LEAH.** My parents loved that old song. Were you named after it?

**ROSE.** Actually, it was named after me.

**LEAH.** What?

**ROSE.** He – Sam wrote the song. About me.

**LEAH.** O.M.G.!

**ROSE.** So I would marry him.

**LEAH.** Get out of here, you wrote that song? My parents love that song! How awesome! You wrote that song?

**ROSE.** About me. All those things in that song, about how beautiful the girl was, with the sweet lips…

**LEAH.** That was some hot love song.

**ROSE.** That was me.

**LEAH.** *(calling to a coworker)* Joey, you won't believe who this is.

**SAM.** No. No, no, no, no. Please. That's all right. That's okay, Joey.

**LEAH.** And you're so modest.

**SAM.** *(modestly)* Oh. Well…

**ROSE.** He's embarrassed. He hasn't written anything since.

**SAM.** I have so. Written other songs.

**ROSE.** Hits. Hit songs.

**LEAH.** Well, I guess if you wrote a song like that, that's enough. Right?

**SAM.** Thank you, Leah. You're very sweet.

**ROSE.** Still, twenty-five years. You know. Not to have another song…

**SAM.** I wrote "Brunch at Katz's."

**ROSE.** I mean, for me, it's enough.

**SAM.** "Lady Liberty."

**ROSE.** We lived very well off that song for twenty-five years. Very well.

**SAM.** "Sunset on the Hudson."

**ROSE.** But Sam, he's embarrassed.

**SAM.** I'm not embarrassed, unless you embarrass me.

**LEAH.** My parents will totally freak when I tell them I met you.

**ROSE.** Did you know Mel Torme sang that song? Earth, Wind, and Fire?

**LEAH.** Ludacris!

**ROSE.** No really. But lately…he sits at the computer and tries to remember some other song he wrote a million years ago.

**LEAH.** You know what? I'm /gonna just…

**SAM.** Rose. This young lady, Leah doesn't need/ to hear…

**ROSE.** I say, "Forget it! Forget that old song!" But no. He sits there, night and day…

**LEAH.** Cool!

**ROSE.** Or that's what he says he's doing, but who really knows, right?

**LEAH.** So, let me get you those brochures

**ROSE.** Do you have a boyfriend, Leah?

**LEAH.** Um, yeah?

**ROSE.** What do you think he's doing right now?

**LEAH.** He works for Virgin Airlines. We actually met when I was…

**ROSE.** That's what he told you, right? That he was going to work today?

**SAM.** Rose, what are you doing?

*(There is an uncomfortable beat.)*

**LEAH.** You know what? I'm going to let you fill this out while I go find those brochures.

**SAM.** Thanks, Leah.

**LEAH.** I think you're going to love this package.

**SAM.** That sounds great.

**LEAH.** Great!

*(She hurries off.* **SAM** *watches her leave.)*

**ROSE.** Pretty girl.

**SAM.** *(annoyed)* What the hell, Rose?

**ROSE.** Don't you think she's pretty?

**SAM.** What's with you today?

**ROSE.** She has nice teeth.

**SAM.** I've written other songs.

**ROSE.** Course she has one of those long thin necks. Makes her look a little pin-headish.

**SAM.** "Throw Your Arms Around the Moon."

**ROSE.** You know who she reminds me of?

**SAM.** No.

**ROSE.** Guess. Guess who she reminds me of.

**SAM.** No!

**ROSE.** Allyson Mendelson.

*(long stunned pause)* She reminds me a bit of Allyson Mendelson.

*(pause)*

**SAM.** How do you know Allyson Mendelson?

**ROSE.** How do *you* know Allyson Mendelson?

   *(pause)*

**SAM.** You've been looking at my computer?

**ROSE.** Facebook. What are you, twelve?

**SAM.** Rose. That's private./ I mean…

**ROSE.** Really? It doesn't seem private. You have one hundred thirty-two friends…

**SAM.** Oh God.

**ROSE.** Who seem to know everything about you. Your minute by minute change of status all through each day while I think you're working on your song. Sam Abrams is eating a pastrami sandwich is somehow worthy of note.

**SAM.** I don't look through any /of your…

**ROSE.** You know everything about me, Sam. I have nothing to hide.

   *(silence)* Nice picture.

**SAM.** *(deeply embarrassed)* Oh God.

**ROSE.** Isn't that one of our wedding photos?

**SAM.** Yeah.

**ROSE.** With me cut out.

**SAM.** Well, it's you know, *my* profile picture, so…

**ROSE.** From twenty-five years ago.

**SAM.** *(sigh)* I can't believe you were spying on me. Looking through my…things.

**ROSE.** Lot of friends you have.

**SAM.** Well…

**ROSE.** All women.

**SAM.** Derek is my friend.

**ROSE.** All women and your brother. Who are those women Sam?

**SAM.** Mostly they're just people I play Scrabulous with. Well, it's called Lexulous now. It's Scrabble really. But there was this copyright lawsuit and …

**ROSE.** All these young women you met playing Scrabble.

**SAM.** Yeah, we just play Scrabble. Mostly. I mean, we don't even chat really. Most of them. I just friended them.

**ROSE.** Friended them.

**SAM.** Silly stuff. You know. I might poke them or throw a snowball or a groundhog or something….

**ROSE.** Poke them.

**SAM.** But we don't even talk. Really. Just on Scrabble. Chat. It's just a game. Really. It's…

**ROSE.** You play Scrabble with Allyson Mendelson?

**SAM.** No! No.

**ROSE.** Because you can't find her.

**SAM.** I don't…I don't even know…If she plays Scrabble.

**ROSE.** Who is she?

**SAM.** She's just this /girl…

**ROSE.** Why are you trying to find her?

**SAM.** I went to high school with. It was…

**ROSE.** Hundreds of messages.

**SAM.** Nothing…really.

**ROSE.** Are you the Allyson Mendelson from Jefferson High?

**SAM.** Yeah. Aw jeez.

**ROSE.** You never mentioned her.

**SAM.** It was…you know. We were teenagers.

**ROSE.** Did you love her?

**SAM.** We were kids! She broke my heart. She hurt me. I wrote her this song…

**ROSE.** Oh my God.

**SAM.** I'm trying to remember this song I'd written…

**ROSE.** It was her song?

**SAM.** Yeah. I thought maybe if I wrote to her…

**ROSE.** It's her song you've been trying to remember?

**SAM.** Rose. It was high school. This is thirty years ago/ we're talking. It was nothing.

**ROSE.** One hundred and eight messages. Asking about her. Looking for her. Is not nothing. Sam.

**SAM.** Yeah.

*(Pause. Admitting:)* Yeah.

**ROSE.** Are you going to meet up with her?

**SAM.** I can't find her.

**ROSE.** But if you found her. What would you do?

**SAM.** I don't know.

**ROSE.** You don't know?

**SAM.** Rose. Come on. Look, let's go home. Let's talk about this at home.

*(He takes her arm.)*

**ROSE.** Don't touch me.

**SAM.** Rose. It's just…It's research.

**ROSE.** That's hilarious. I'm off at the shop, I think you're working on your damn song…

**SAM.** I am working on the song. This is part of it.

**ROSE.** Boy, am I an idiot. You're playing games.

**SAM.** No.

**ROSE.** Writing to girls.

**SAM.** No. No, I'm just…I'm trying…

**ROSE.** What?

**SAM.** I'm stuck. Rose. I'm stuck. Everything I write now…. It's bullshit. I can't write anything…true anymore. I can't feel anything true.

*(He sighs deeply.)* I'm trying to remember…what I was like…what it felt like…

**ROSE.** To be hurt?

**SAM.** To be…

**ROSE.** I'll hurt you with that lamp.

**SAM.** Come on, honey.

**ROSE.** Why can't you remember what it's like with me?

**SAM.** We've been together for so long.

**ROSE.** Twenty-five years.

**SAM.** It's not the same now. Of course it isn't.

**ROSE.** It's the same for me.

**SAM.** As when we first met? Come on.

**ROSE.** I still love you as much as when we first met. More. I love you more.

**SAM.** I love you. Honey. It's just…that huge feeling…I'm trying to remember that huge painful, frantic…

**ROSE.** Lust. What you feel for Allyson Mendelson. For all these young women. They're everywhere. I hate them. All these /stupid young…

**SAM.** It's not about the women! Rose. I'm trying to wake up.

**ROSE.** Oh. So playing Scrabble/ on Facebook…

**SAM.** It's all…deadened. Don't you feel that? Like we're under water. I go to sleep deadened every night. And I wake up with my heart pounding, that it's all behind us. That it's all over. Every great, thrilling thing that was going to happen to me, to us, every surprise, has happened already.

**ROSE.** That's nuts. You *make* thrilling things happen.

**SAM.** I have to do this Rose. Somehow. I have to make something. Feel something. Big. Before it's all gone. I have to find this song. Write this song.

**ROSE.** Why don't you just get a red convertible? Why don't you ride around in a leather jacket with the top down? Pretend you're young again.

**SAM.** Don't make fun of me.

*(long pause)*

**ROSE.** I could have married Richard Miller you know.

**SAM.** *(sigh)* I know.

**ROSE.** He was nuts about me. Lusted after me. Big time. I didn't have to marry you, you know.

**SAM.** I know.

**ROSE.** There were plenty of guys.

**SAM.** Richard Miller.

**ROSE.** And others. He was a looker. He had a nice head of hair. Richard Miller.

**SAM.** I had a nice head of hair twenty-five years ago too.

**ROSE.** I remember once he took me to the park. We rented one of those boats in the park. I was wearing this / little pink skirt.

**SAM.** *(said in unison with her)* Little pink skirt.

**ROSE.** So romantic. He was crazy about me.

**SAM.** I was crazy about you...am.

**ROSE.** When we broke up he moved to Italy. Can you imagine? How heartbroken he must have been? To have to move that far away?

**SAM.** I thought he had a job there...

**ROSE.** To have to move so far away to try to forget the pain? Everything he saw must have hurt him – reminded him of the times we'd spent together. And now he had to go on without me.

**SAM.** You told me that he got a /job in...

**ROSE.** I could have been living in Italy if I'd stayed with him. I could be sitting in a travel agency in Rome right now. Who knows where I could have gone. What I would have done with my life if I'd stayed with him. *(with growing fury)* But you wrote that damn song! You tricked me into marrying you!

**SAM.** I tricked you? Rose...

**ROSE.** If I'd known what would happen. If I'd known you'd be writing to other girls. Allyson Mendelson...

**SAM.** Rosie.

**ROSE.** I would have told you where to put that song.

*(During this* **LEAH** *starts toward them, hears the discussion and slinks back away.)*

**SAM.** *(Looking around. Everyone is watching them.)* Let's go home.

*(pause)*

**ROSE.** Maybe I'll go on Facebook. How about that? Maybe I'll do a MySpace. How would you like that? If you looked at my computer and I was poking Richard Miller?

**SAM.** I would think you were trying to remember what it was like to be eighteen again. And that that was your …touchstone to remember it.

**ROSE.** My ass. You'd be worried sick.

**SAM.** Okay.

**ROSE.** Jealous sick.

**SAM.** Okay.

*(pause)*

**ROSE.** Or you wouldn't. That's how bad it is. You wouldn't.

*(They sit in silence for a moment.)*

I want you to give it up.

**SAM.** What?

**ROSE.** All of it. Facebook. Scrabble. Allyson Mendelson.

**SAM.** Well…I'm in the middle of games. I can't just…

**ROSE.** You are out of your mind!!! When we get home I want you to delete it from your computer.

**SAM.** I will. Once I…I'm trying to write the song. It's helping Rose. It's helping me remember.

**ROSE.** No. Forget the damn song. Forget it. Delete them.

**SAM.** I…will. You just have to give me…a little time. To…

**ROSE.** To what? Time to what, Sam?

**SAM.** To say goodbye. OK? Just let me…tell them goodbye.

*(Pause. **LEAH** returns cautiously and sits across from them again.)*

**LEAH.** So…I found those brochures.

**SAM.** *(can't even look at her)* Yeah. You know, maybe this isn't a good time.

**ROSE.** The hell it isn't. Give me those brochures. We're going on that fucking cruise.

## Scene Two

*(The ship. **ROSE** and **SAM** are standing at the ship railing, looking out on the Mediterranean. Everything is a brilliant blue. But somehow they still seem small and gray. **SAM** is trying very hard.)*

**ROSE.** Isn't it gorgeous? It's so blue.

**SAM.** It is…incredibly blue.

**ROSE.** It's blue like in the brochures.

**SAM.** You're right, Rosie. It really is. It's very, very…blue.

**ROSE.** Aren't you glad we came?

**SAM.** Of course. This was a great idea. I'm really glad we did this. Really glad.

*(He puts his arm around her and gives her a kiss on the cheek. She is delighted.)*

**ROSE.** This is so great! Here! Together!

**SAM.** *(happy for her happiness)* It is, honey. It's great.

**ROSE.** Maybe I'll sell the shop!

**SAM.** What??

**ROSE.** Maybe I'll sell it. And then we'll be completely free. To…you know…

**SAM.** But…

**ROSE.** Travel, or…

**SAM.** But you…

**ROSE.** We could travel and…do whatever. Whatever we want.

**SAM.** …you love the shop.

**ROSE.** Well, it was good because I could be home with Barry. When he was little.

**SAM.** But…But…

**ROSE.** Make my own hours.

**SAM.** But you…you love…

**ROSE.** I love to travel!

**SAM.** The shop…

**ROSE.** Nobody really knits any more. It's a generation of non-knitters.

**SAM.** That's not true. You were telling me the other day… about /that group of…

**ROSE.** I'm going to do it.

**SAM.** Girls. Young girls who came in.

**ROSE.** I'm going to do it, Sam.

**SAM.** To learn…to…

**ROSE.** I'm going to sell the shop.

**SAM.** to…knit.

**ROSE.** I am. And then we can be free.

*(beat)*

**SAM.** Ok, honey. Whatever you want.

*(We hear a thread of music.* **SAM** *is distracted away by a bikini-clad woman passing by them. He begins humming to himself, a little desperately.* **ROSE** *takes this in. Determined:)*

**ROSE.** We've got the late seating tonight.

**SAM.** Oh?

**ROSE.** I thought, for our celebration, tonight it would be nice to have the late seating.

**SAM.** Good thinking.

**ROSE.** And there will probably be a cake, though I'm not saying for sure.

**SAM.** That's nice.

**ROSE.** I switched with the Morganthals. That was nice of them, don't you think? To switch with us?

**SAM.** Very nice.

*(pause)*

**ROSE.** You wish you were home.

**SAM.** No!

**ROSE.** You wish you were back at your computer. Talking with other people. People you don't even know. You're trapped here with me. And three thousand other people. But really you're trapped here with me.

**SAM.** Honey, what are you talking about?

**ROSE.** I love you, Sam. I never stopped loving you.

**SAM.** I love you, too.

**ROSE.** But, I don't want to just be tolerated for the next… however many years I've got left. I deserve better than that.

**SAM.** Rose, I don't just tolerate you. You're my best friend.

**ROSE.** I'm your *only* friend. That you actually *know*.

**SAM.** I came here. Because you wanted me to. I'm here. I'm here with you.

**ROSE.** No you're not. I'm alone. Like always.

**SAM.** What are you talking about, Rosie?

**ROSE.** Since Barry left. It's just me.

**SAM.** I'm with you all the time. When you're not working, we're constantly together.

**ROSE.** That's what it feels like. To you.

**SAM.** That's what it is.

**ROSE.** What am I supposed to do now? I did it. He's grown up. He's a nice boy. He's off on his own.

**SAM.** He'll be back. For visits.

**ROSE.** I don't have a song that I have to write. Barry. He was my song. Done.

*(silence)*

**SAM.** So keep the shop.

**ROSE.** No!

**SAM.** Ok! Then you could take an art class. Or…scrapbooking? Wasn't that what Peggy was doing?

**ROSE.** Glue things into a book. That's what you think I should be doing. For the next forty years.

**SAM.** Peggy seems happy.

**ROSE.** You don't know me at all. Do you?

**SAM.** Sure I do.

**ROSE.** Forty years. If we're lucky. Forty years left.

**SAM.** God.

**ROSE.** Forty years gluing things into a book so that I remember them. And then what?

*(silence)* I want to be adored. Like my song.

**SAM.** Well...

**ROSE.** Why don't you adore me any more? Why don't you look at me and want to write your song?

**SAM.** I don't know. I'm sorry. I don't know how to feel that way any more.

**ROSE.** I would be a lot of things for you Sam, I would. But I can't be twenty-five again.

**SAM.** I don't want you to be.

**ROSE.** And you're not either you know. If those women you played Scrabble with...they think you look like your wedding picture.

**SAM.** No. I know. Believe me. They take one look at me, and they're horrified.

**ROSE.** What?

**SAM.** What?

**ROSE.** They take one look at you?

**SAM.** Oh. Well...

**ROSE.** You've met them?

**SAM.** No, but that's what I'm saying. No.

**ROSE.** What?

**SAM.** I mean...just for coffee.

**ROSE.** WHAT???

**SAM.** Just a few of them. Who live in New York. I'd just... You know...we'd meet for coffee.

**ROSE.** Oh my God.

**SAM.** But...like you said. I mean, they're expecting the Facebook guy to show up. They take one look at me...

**ROSE.** You've been meeting with these women?

**SAM.** No! No, not at all. Not, not any more Rose. I mean... it was nothing. Coffee. That's all.

**ROSE.** That's it.

**SAM.** Rosie. No.

**ROSE.** That's IT!

**SAM.** Nothing ever…

**ROSE.** I don't want to know. I don't want to know what you did. I don't want to hear what you hoped might happen with these women.
*(beat)* WHAT DID YOU HOPE MIGHT HAPPEN WITH THESE WOMEN???

No. I don't even want to know. It's over. You've flushed twenty-five years down the toilet.

**SAM.** Rosie. Don't say that.

**ROSE.** I mean it. I'm through. You have betrayed me.

**SAM.** I didn't. This is what I'm saying. I never did. Anything. I wouldn't have done…

*(Suddenly, there is the most beautiful music ever played, heard only by* **SAM***. It is his song. It may be singing. It may be a harp. It may be the eerie, sad sound of the theremin.* **SAM** *is completely enthralled.* **ROSE** *continues to yell at him but he can't even hear her now.)*

**ROSE.** I'll never be able to look at you the same way again.

*(But he can hear nothing but the music. It fills him with all the longing and feeling he's been searching for. And she is so caught up in what she's saying that she doesn't notice he is gone.)*

You have your faults, Sam. God knows. God KNOWS you have your faults. But I hold my tongue. I'm not one to count grievances. Even though you're self-centered, and moody, and helpless around the house and…

*(The music swells, and we can only hear bits of what she says, while* **SAM** *hears none of it. He is trying to hum along.)*

you have to be told to put your clothes in the hamper after twenty-five fucking years. What the hell! PUT YOUR FUCKING CLOTHES IN THE HAMPER! But this? Forget it. It's over.

*(The music fades out)*

The marriage is over.

**SAM.** *(coming back)* Did you hear that?

**ROSE.** What?

**SAM.** That was it. That was my song. Oh my God.

*(**ROSE** stares at him stunned.)*

*(He tries to hum it but it's already lost to him.)*

How did it go, Rose? Oh shit – it's already gone… Do you remember how it went?

**ROSE.** Oh. My. God.

**SAM.** What?

**ROSE.** *(furious)* Oh my God! I cannot believe…

**SAM.** Rose, don't you understand? That was my song. Didn't you hear it?

**ROSE.** Did you hear ME? CAN you hear me??? I said I'm through! Our marriage is over.

*(The music swells up again and **SAM** is again transported by it.)*

I gave up all my good years on you. My attractive years. The years I might have had a chance to find someone else. Someone to really love me.

*(**SAM** is completely swept away. He begins to climb up the railing.)*

**ROSE.** What are you doing? Sam? Don't be an idiot. Get down from there.

**SAM.** I have to remember. Help me. Help me remember.

**ROSE.** Get down off there.

**SAM.** That's the most…Oh God. That's the most beautiful…

*(And he jumps overboard.)*

**ROSE.** SAM!!!

*(Blackout. We hear the splash.)*

HELP!!! Someone…Help! Man…Man overboard!!! HELP!

*(We hear **ROSE** continue to call for help. And the commotion that that creates.)*

## Scene Three

*(Lights up on a small island in the Mediterranean. Saturated with brilliant light and color.)*

*(SAM is lying where he was beached, on a rock, unconscious, drying in the sun. There are bones and fragments of clothes along the shore. Also bits of luggage and small treasures – the debris of thousands of years of mortality.)*

*(On another rock sits the SIREN. She is sublimely lovely. She sits madly playing a hand-held solitaire game, frantically pushing the buttons.)*

*(SAM stirs. Looks around. Disoriented.)*

**SAM.** *(coughing)* Ooof. My back. Ow. Where am I?

*(The SIREN shushes him, sharply.)*

Oh my God!!! Allyson?

**SIREN.** Zeus Almighty.

**SAM.** Allyson, you're here. What are you...?
*(suddenly disoriented)* Wait...where are we? Am I...dead?

**SIREN.** Are you? You were supposed to perish. Did you perish?

**SAM.** Did I...?

**SIREN.** You are not allowed to talk if you are dead.

**SAM.** Uhhhh...

**SIREN.** You are not dead.
*(to the Gods)* Was he sent by Zeus? Hades? Where did you come from?

**SAM.** ...The Carnival Cruise?

**SIREN.** Ughh. Another jumper. I hate when this happens. It is so off-story.

**SAM.** Wait...Are you Allyson Mendelson?

**SIREN.** Is she a great and powerful emissary of the Gods?

**SAM.** No. She's a girl from Teaneck.

**SIREN.** Then, no.

**SAM.** You look so much like her. It's unbelievable.

**SIREN.** Yeah, well…you want me to look like her.

**SAM.** What is this place?

**SIREN.** Anthemusa.

**SAM.** I don't think that was on the itinerary.

**SIREN.** It is my island. You are on my island.

**SAM.** Oh God. I jumped, right? Overboard? And swam here?

**SIREN.** You were supposed to perish.

*(indicating the bones and human remains)*

**SAM.** *(horrified)* All those people died here?

**SIREN.** *(looking at him sternly)* No, most of them washed up dead like the story says. Come on, try again. Go back out, and this time, do not make it.

**SAM.** I'm sorry, Miss. I'm very confused.

**SIREN.** Well, you could just wait here and languish. But that would be long and awful. If you choose, you can touch me…

*(She plucks a flower near her rock and all the leaves fall off, or it wilts away.)*

And we can get it over with quickly. But it has to be your choice.

**SAM.** I think I've been out in the sun too long. I don't feel so well. Is there anything to drink?

*(She indicates the ocean.)*

That's ocean water. That would kill me.

**SIREN.** Ok.

**SAM.** *(standing stiffly)* Oof. I must have swum for hours. What was I thinking?

**SIREN.** You followed the song.

**SAM.** The song! Yes! You heard it too? Do you remember? How it goes?

**SIREN.** Yes.

**SAM.** You do? Can you sing it?

**SIREN.** No.

**SAM.** Can you... Can you hum it? Anything?

**SIREN.** No.

**SAM.** Come on. Please?

**SIREN.** No. Look, are you going to touch me and get this over with? Or do you want a slow painful death?

**SAM.** I don't want any death. I want to remember.

**SIREN.** Slow and painful then. Suit yourself.

*(He stares at her for a moment.)*

**SAM.** You're so beautiful...it hurts.

**SIREN.** Yeah. That is my thing.

*(She goes back to madly pushing the buttons. He tries to hum. Starting to get it.)*

**SAM.** I'm remembering. Here with you...It'll come back.

*(She wins her game. The horn sounds and applause from the little box.)*

What are you doing? What is that?

**SIREN.** *(finally enjoying the conversation.)* This is my magic box. It was a gift from the Gods! It washed up on shore one day. There are all these numbered boxes, see? And if you put them in just the right order, you triumph.

**SAM.** It's solitaire.

**SIREN.** I am very good. I always triumph. Always. And when I do the Gods rejoice – a little horn sounds and the boxes jump all over the square. It is wonderfully diverting. I cannot seem to do it enough. It is just so wonderfully diverting.

*(There is the sound of a ship's horn in the distance. She sighs.)*

Oh. Wait.

*(The **SIREN** sings the eerie, beautiful song of the **SIREN**. It is breathtaking. **SAM** rises in awe. She sings for a moment and then there is the sound of a ship crashing in the distance. Distant screams. She stops singing and goes back to her solitaire game.)*

**SIREN.** *(cont.)* You probably wonder if every game is winnable. It seems like it would all depend on the layout of the little numbered boxes. But now that I have become an expert…

*(She holds up the game for a moment.)*

Right here. See? It says I am an expert. Now I always triumph.

**SAM.** *(stunned)* That was it – my song for Allyson. How do you know that song?

**SIREN.** Sorry, but that is my song.

**SAM.** No, no, no. That was it. Sing it again.

**SIREN.** I sing it when the boats come.

**SAM.** It's…it's the most…

**SIREN.** …beautiful thing you have ever heard. Yeah. Here – see my stats? They are very high. I am very very good.

**SAM.** Oh God. I felt it. When you sang. Young. Like I could write again.

*(He tries humming it, but again, can't remember the song.)*

Why can't I get it? What's wrong with me?

**SIREN.** It is not your song. It has been my song for like, thousands of years. I came with that song.

**SAM.** Thousands of…

**SIREN.** When the boat comes I sing that song, and then the men steer the boat into those jagged rocks where it is torn asunder and they perish.

**SAM.** Oh no! Did the boat I was on – did that boat crash?

**SIREN.** When you jumped off they must have been distracted. I want to make that clear.

*(to the Gods)* They did not resist me. He distracted them.

**SAM.** It didn't crash?

**SIREN.** No. That was very bad of you.

**SAM.** Thank God! Rose is on that boat. Ohhhh. Rose. She's gotta be pretty pissed.

**SIREN.** Why, did she want the boat to crash?

**SAM.** No. We were on our anniversary cruise. She was talking to me, and I jumped. Overboard. And swam away. From her. That's not good.

**SIREN.** You chose the song.

**SAM.** No. I just…I lost my head for a minute. I…I love my wife.

**SIREN.** Uh huh.

**SAM.** I do. I love her. But passion…

**SIREN.** Yeah?

**SAM.** That kind of passion, doesn't last.

**SIREN.** What does it do?

**SAM.** It fades. It turns into something…else.

**SIREN.** What does it turn into?

**SAM.** Comfort, I guess.

**SIREN.** And that is bad.

**SAM.** No. Unless you want passion. You are young. You don't know about all that yet.

**SIREN.** I know that passion crashes the boats.

**SAM.** Why do you sing to crash the boats?

**SIREN.** It is my part of the story.

**SAM.** What story?

**SIREN.** *(exasperated sigh)* My boss, Demeter? Her daughter, Persephone was stolen by Hades.

**SAM.** Wait, this sounds very familiar.

**SIREN.** We were sent to rescue her but there were…complications. Long story short, my boss is seeking revenge on man.

**SAM.** And now you just stay here and lure people to their deaths?

**SIREN.** Men. They cannot resist me. They can tie themselves to the mast, or they can put wax in their ears, but if they hear one note, they go mad with passion.

**SAM.** That's terrible. Sing it again.

**SIREN.** No.

**SAM.** Please.

**SIREN.** Nope.

**SAM.** I…I need to hear it. And then I'll remember. Just once more.

**SIREN.** Uh uh.

**SAM.** I'll do…whatever. I'll give you…whatever. Whatever you ask.

**SIREN.** Your life?

**SAM.** What?

**SIREN.** Will you give up your life?

**SAM.** Of course not!

**SIREN.** Come on. And then I get my kill before the sun sets.

**SAM.** No!

**SIREN.** Look at me.

**SAM.** No!

**SIREN.** I am Allyson! You can touch me. Have me. However you want.

**SAM.** I can?

**SIREN.** Yes. And then you die!

**SAM.** I don't want to die.

**SIREN.** OH MY ZEUS! CAN YOU HEAR ME?? YOU ARE GOING TO DIE. DO YOU WANT TO DIE IN ECSTACY OR DO YOU WANT TO DIE IN AGONY???

**SAM.** You sound a lot more like Rose than Allyson.

**SIREN.** Look. We are way off story. You were supposed to die at sea. I am offering you one great moment of passion. Ok? It is like…a bonus game! Come. Sweetheart. Did she call you sweetheart?

**SAM.** No.

**SIREN.** What did she call you?

**SAM.** …Sam?

**SIREN.** Sam. Come to me, Sam. Touch me.

**SAM.** How can I touch you?

**SIREN.** Any way you want.

**SAM.** All over?

**SIREN.** Sure.

**SAM.** How long before I die?

**SIREN.** You will have enough time. Do not worry.

**SAM.** *(He looks at the skeletons along the shore.)* All these men chose that? They gave up everything for that one moment?

**SIREN.** *(seductively)* It was worth it. I will make it worth it.

**SAM.** You look so much like her. Your hair, your lips, your arms, your…

**SIREN.** *(trying various seductive poses)* Come here.

**SAM.** What would Rose think?

**SIREN.** She will never know. Come.

**SAM.** But I'll know.

**SIREN.** Come here. Sam.

**SAM.** Ohhh…

**SIREN.** Touch me.

**SAM.** You're so beautiful.

**SIREN.** Yes.

**SAM.** I do want you.

**SIREN.** Of course you do. Give in.

**SAM.** Yes.

**SIREN.** Come to me.

**SAM.** Is this what I want?

**SIREN.** Of course it is. Touch me.

**SAM.** Oooo.

**SIREN.** I am Allyson.

**SAM.** I want…I want to write my song. How often do the boats come?

**SIREN.** What??

**SAM.** When the next boat comes, you'll sing again?

**SIREN.** Yes…

**SAM.** I'll just wait. Thanks. For you to sing again. Ok? I'll just wait. *(He curls up to fall asleep.)*

**SIREN.** *(disgusted, to the Gods)* Humans.

*(She returns to her game.)*

*(The lights shift. The sun sets and rises. The* **SIREN** *continues playing her game.)*

*(***SAM** *wakens. Groans.)*

**SAM.** Ohhh. I'm so thirsty.

**SIREN.** You are *still* alive?

**SAM.** I'm going to die if I don't get water.

**SIREN.** Ok.

*(He groans.)*

You have not even looked for some. You are not very resourceful.

**SAM.** No. You're right.

*(He groans.)*

**SIREN.** Do you always do this? Lie around and groan when you want something?

**SAM.** *(getting up, painfully)* I guess I do.

*(He begins walking around the island.)*

I guess Rose just gets it for me.

**SIREN.** She must be having the time of her life right now. Without you groaning nearby.

**SAM.** I imagine she's heartbroken.

**SIREN.** Heartbroken. You are hilarious.

**SAM.** That is what Rose always says! She says I'm hilarious. But really she means I'm annoying.

**SIREN.** Yeah? That is what I mean too. How does she bear it? Does she put wax in her ears?

**SAM.** No.

**SIREN.** She can probably leave for big blocks of time. I imagine that helps.

**SAM.** She doesn't want to though. She wants to be with me. All the time.

**SIREN.** Is she simple-minded?

**SAM.** No. She loves me.

**SIREN.** Why?

**SAM.** I don't know.

**SIREN.** Is it passion?

**SAM.** It's a good question really. She just always wants me around.

**SIREN.** She needs a box with numbers.

**SAM.** Why does she love me?

**SIREN.** It is a mystery.

**SAM.** It really takes very little to make her happy. She wants me to put my clothes in the laundry basket. She wants to travel. She wants me to stop looking away. Look at her.

*(having walked all the way around and back again)*

This is a very small island. There's nothing. No water.

**SIREN.** Yeah. I did not think so.

**SAM.** I'm going to die.

**SIREN.** You think?

**SAM.** Oh my God. I'm going to die. I am. I'm really going to die.

**SIREN.** I thought we had established that!

**SAM.** I can't die here.

Help me. Come back to New York with me.

**SIREN.** New York?

**SAM.** My island. If you came to New York, if you sang our song, we would be a massive big deal.

**SIREN.** I am a massive big deal here.

**SAM.** Well, here. Yeah. But – big fish, little pond, you know?

**SIREN.** It is the Mediterranean.

**SAM.** But, with our song, and your voice…

**SIREN.** Yeah. See, that is not what I do. I sing my song and the boats crash. That is what I do.

*(beat)* And now I honor the Gods with my triumph on the magic box.

**SAM.** That's all you want out of life? That's what you want your legacy to be?

**SIREN.** Legacy…

**SAM.** What you leave behind.

**SIREN.** What do you do that is so important?

**SAM.** *(a little embarrassed)* I'm a…song writer.

**SIREN.** What is that?

**SAM.** I write songs. That people sing. I write some songs that people sing. I wrote one song that people sing. Rose Adelle?

**SIREN.** Never heard of it.

**SAM.** It is very famous. I mean, most people…

**SIREN.** I never heard of it.

**SAM.** So anyway, that's what I do.

**SIREN.** So…I guess that is way more important than what I do.

**SAM.** No.

**SIREN.** I can see why you would swim to my island and judge how what I do is so much less important than what you do on your island.

**SAM.** I didn't mean that.

**SIREN.** That is a huge — what did you call it? Legacy? That is a huge legacy you made. Very impressive legacy.

**SAM.** No. I know.

**SIREN.** You are a big fish, I guess. In your big pond.

**SAM.** No. I'm nothing. You're right. I'm leaving nothing behind when I die. A song? A son who doesn't want to visit me? A wife…a wife that I've hurt.

**SIREN.** You jumped overboard.

**SAM.** I did.

*(We hear a ship's horn in the distance.)*

**SIREN.** Wait.

*(She sings again. Again we hear a ship crash off in the distance. The screams are a bit louder this time. The **SIREN** goes back to her game.)*

**SAM.** *(He tries, unsuccessfully, to hum it. Miserable)* It's gone. And those screams. You just killed all those people.

**SIREN.** Uh huh.

*(She is back to frantically moving the cards. Then there is the sound of a trumpet and applause from the box. The SIREN looks up triumphantly.)*

See? Told you. I won. I always win.

*(to the Gods)* That one was for you!

**SAM.** Oh God. I'm a fool. I'm going to die here. I'm such a fool.

*(SAM crumples into a ball. The sun sets. And rises.)*

*(SAM is mumbling in his sleep. Singing pieces of Rose Adelle.)*

Rose...Rosie.

*(SAM wakens, dazed and looks to the rock, but now it is ROSE sitting there instead of the Siren. ROSE is in her 70's and is knitting.)*

**SAM.** Rose!

**ROSE.** Is that how you say it? Epiphone? You know – the fancy guitar he's been wanting?

**SAM.** The what?

**ROSE.** *(exasperated)* Oh my God. Have you been listening to me? Sam?

**SAM.** Rose. I'm so happy to see you.

*(He goes to her and is about to throw his arms around her.)*

Can I touch you?

**ROSE.** Can you what?

**SAM.** Oh, I don't even care.

*(He throws his arms around her.)*

**ROSE.** *(She is surprised but pleased.)* Crazy. Look, I know it's expensive and Stephanie will throw a fit.

**SAM.** Stephanie...

**ROSE.** But she won't be happy whatever we do. And how often does a boy turn sixteen.

**SAM.** Sixteen?

**ROSE.** *(loudly)* Do you have your hearing aids in?

**SAM.** What?

**ROSE.** *(even louder and exasperated)* Sam. For God's sakes, GO PUT IN YOUR HEARING AIDS.

**SAM.** You're so old. But you're Rose.

**ROSE.** Great. Thanks.

**SAM.** You're wonderful.

**ROSE.** *(very pleased)* Yeah? You think it's a good idea?

**SAM.** You always have good ideas. If I just listen to you.

**ROSE.** Stephanie wants Tom to earn the money himself if he wants a fancy guitar.

**SAM.** Tom.

**ROSE.** I told Barry, "Look. This is the grandparents' prerogative. To spoil the grandchildren. My parents did it. You'll do it."

**SAM.** Grandparents…

**ROSE.** That's what I told him.

**SAM.** We're grandparents.

**ROSE.** Are you following what I'm saying, Sam???

**SAM.** Yes, sweetheart. So we'll get the guitar.

**ROSE.** He has that concert coming up. Or gig. He loves to say gig. He's adorable.

**SAM.** Yes.

**ROSE.** I think we give it to him there. Have the band play "Happy Birthday." We present it to him. And then he plays the new guitar – at the gig!

**SAM.** That seems a little overboard.

**ROSE.** It's not.

**SAM.** To make such a big show in front of…

**ROSE.** It's good. It'll be fine. It's his sixteenth birthday. It's special.

**SAM.** You have to *make* thrilling things happen.

**ROSE.** You only live once.

**SAM.** Hey, I'm going to write a song! For Tom! For his birthday!

**ROSE.** That's a great idea!

**SAM.** Tell me about him. Tom.

**ROSE.** Tell you about him? What are you, nuts?

**SAM.** You know, describe him. For the song, I mean.

**ROSE.** Well, Stephanie says he's just like you.

**SAM.** She does?

**ROSE.** Of course she does! And she's none too happy about it!

**SAM.** He's just like me. Tom. My grandson. I love you, Rose.

**ROSE.** Good.

**SAM.** I want to get old with you.

**ROSE.** Too late.

*(They both laugh again.)*

*(There is the sound of a boat off in the distance.)*

Oh. Wait.

*(And* **ROSE** *sings her song. Rose Adelle.* **SAM** *enjoys it. And the boat doesn't crash. He sits back and closes his eyes and listens to her sing.)*

*(And she slowly walks off, and is replaced by the* **SIREN**. **SAM** *is quite hallucinatory by now.)*

**SAM.** Rose?

**SIREN.** Nope.

**SAM.** Rose, is that you?

**SIREN.** No.

**SAM.** Are you sure...

**SIREN.** Go back to sleep.

**SAM.** I remember when we met, Rose. You were wearing that pink skirt. We went on a little boat. In Central Park. No. Wait. That was Allyson. In the pink skirt? No. That was you, Rose. But it wasn't me. Who was it?
*(very frightened)* I can't remember. Which one were you? Which one was I?

**SIREN.** Wow. You are really losing it.

*(to the Gods)* Not long now I would say.

**SAM.** Rose. You were the one.

*(starting to weep)* Why did I jump? You were so beautiful in your pink skirt, Rose. Why didn't I kiss you?

*(Three little beeps come from the square box.)*

**SIREN.** What was that?

**SAM.** What was that?

**SIREN.** Are you talking to me little box? What are you saying?

**SAM.** *(coming out of it, seeing the* **SIREN***)* Oh, it's you.

**SIREN.** Shhh. My box from the Gods is talking to me.

**SAM.** You don't look like Allyson any more.

**SIREN.** I do not?

*(The box beeps again.)*

What does it mean?

*(to the Gods)* What does it mean?

**SAM.** The batteries are running out.

**SIREN.** What are the batteries?

**SAM.** They're little cylinders full of power. But you have to change them. Or recharge them.

**SIREN.** I do?

**SAM.** Yeah, they don't last forever.

**SIREN.** Oh no. The game will stop playing?

**SAM.** You're going to need more batteries.

**SIREN.** *(thoroughly frantic)* What will I do? I cannot just wait for the boats any more! I got used to the game. It is so diverting! I need the game!

**SAM.** Look, I need to get back. Back to my wife.

**SIREN.** What do I do?

**SAM.** Let me get to the next boat and if I survive, I'll bring you back some batteries.

**SIREN.** How will you get to a boat?

**SAM.** Just don't sing. Once.

**SIREN.** I cannot do that.

**SAM.** Just once. Break the rules.

**SIREN.** You are just trying to trick me.

**SAM.** Please let me go.

**SIREN.** Hey. Why can you not just change your batteries. Recharge your batteries?

**SAM.** Recharge my batteries. People can't...

**SIREN.** Hah! I knew you were lying. The Gods would not give me a box that died.

*(It beeps three times again. The sound of bwa bwa bwa bwa as it dies. Its light goes out. The SIREN stares at it in terror. Presses the buttons. Nothing happens. The game has died. Greek tragedy.)*

Noooooooooooooooooooooo!

*(The SIREN madly presses the buttons. Shakes the machine. Rattles it against her ear.)*

NO NO NO NO! It is dead. Noooooooooooo.

*(She hits it.)* Stop it! Stop being dead.

*(There is a boat horn off in the distance.)*

Oh no. No no no. I cannot sing. But I must sing.

*(And she does. The eerie, beautiful song. But now it has a heartbreaking minor key. It is the saddest sound ever heard. But still it works. We hear the ship crash in the distance. The screams are painfully loud this time.)*

**SAM.** *(covering his ears)* Stop. Stop!

*(She has stopped. She is softly weeping to herself.)*

**SIREN.** No more little numbered boxes. No more stats. No more triumph. This is what death is? Death is terrible. You spoke the truth. You see the future.

**SAM.** I do. Let me get to the ship.

**SIREN.** It is not in the story.

**SAM.** The story isn't over. We can change the story.

**SIREN.** Change the story?

**SAM.** I can see it. This is the next part.

**SIREN.** You will get me batteries?

**SAM.** Yeah. Look. See this little compartment here? This is where you put them. The plus goes this way and the minus goes that way.

**SIREN.** And the game will live again?

**SAM.** Yes. The game will live.

*(There is a ship's horn.)*

Don't sing, all right? Let me get to the boat. And I'll get you the batteries.

*(He dives into the water.)*

**SIREN.** Go forth. Do not die. Get me the batteries!

*(Lights fade.)*

## Scene Four

*(Lights up on* **ROSE**, *in her apartment. She is dressed in black. She is holding the phone and pacing. All the time, knitting and knitting. Finally she consults a scrap of paper and dials.)*

**ROSE.** Richard? Oh my God. It's Rosie! Rosie Abrams…or Jacobs. Was. Rosie Jacobs. Hi. Yeah. I know. How are you?

Wow, how exciting. What's her name?

Caroline. Nice. Where was the wedding?

Oh, you live on Long Island? No, I know you live on Long Island. I called Long Island. I'm sorry. I'm a little nervous. So was it beautiful? Did you walk her down the aisle?

Ah. Our son, Barry…yeah, I married Sam. Sam Abrams? He was in your dorm? Yeah…so, did you marry an Italian girl?

Oh. I'm so sorry. How awful. Yeah…. I…umm…lost… Sam…too.

No, no. It was a boating…thing. An incident, a boating…incident. Yeah. Actually, it was recent. I'm…it's terrible, I'm sure it looks terrible, me calling you…it was very recent, very very recent, and I was, I mean, I'm in…mourning, or…but I was thinking about you. I mean before this happened and…Well, that's sounds awful too, right? God.

I found you on Facebook. You know, I was checking Sam's accounts to make sure…anyway, Mimi Glazer is a friend of his and a friend of yours, so I could see your info as a…friend of a friend. It's all so weird. God what a world, right.

Richard. It's really good to talk to you. I kind of can't believe it. I really needed to hear…an old friend. I've been so…

Friday? I would like that, I would. But I think it's too soon. I'm still so…

*(The doorbell rings.)* Oh, could you hold on a sec.

*(She opens the door.* **SAM** *stands there, dishevelled but grinning.)*

**SAM.** Honey, I'm home!

*(**ROSE** stands with the phone, paralyzed.)*

I survived!

*(She doesn't respond.)*

I made it back! To you!!

*(still nothing)*

I'm so sorry. I realized. I've been an idiot. I've been a complete fool. I want to be with you. I do. I want to write my song for you. I want to be here for you.

*(He goes to her, to hug her, but she backs away stunned.)*

Rosie?

*(She remembers the phone.)*

**ROSE.** Ummm…someone's at the door. So…You know what? Friday would be great. 7. Great. I'll see you then Richard. Miller.

*(She hangs up. Blackout.)*

## Scene Five

*(Friday night. ROSE is getting ready for her date. She stands in her slip, pinning up her hair as SAM watches. She is nervous and having difficulty getting it right.)*

SAM. So did the girl come? What was her name? Stephanie?

ROSE. Courtney.

SAM. Right. She came? That's nice. What was she like?

ROSE. It wasn't really the occasion. To get to know her.

SAM. No. Right. How did he look?

ROSE. Well…his father had just committed suicide by jumping off a cruise ship in order to escape his mother… so…let's see…he looked…traumatized. He looked a lot like me.

SAM. I'm so sorry, Rose.

ROSE. Yeah.

SAM. It was nice that he came back. Right?

ROSE. You were dead. What do you think he'd do? Send a postcard?

SAM. Right.

ROSE. Of course, now I know you have to die for him to come home….

*(She looks at him evilly.)*

SAM. Did they seem good together? Is she good to him?

ROSE. She doesn't cut off his crusts.

SAM. No?

ROSE. He says he makes his own sandwiches. Apparently women don't make men sandwiches any more. Apparently we're throwbacks. Apparently men of your generation make their own damn sandwiches.

SAM. I could do that. Make sandwiches.

*(ROSE laughs bitterly.)*

I could. I will. You just always did it so well that…but I will.

So, what do you think you'll have?

**ROSE.** What?

**SAM.** Tonight. They have good eggplant parmesan there. Remember? When we had the eggplant parmesan?

**ROSE.** No.

**SAM.** Last time we were there…. Didn't we have the…

**ROSE.** You had the eggplant parmesan. I had the gnocchi.

**SAM.** Oh. Right.

*(pause)* So, you could have the gnocchi. Again.

**ROSE.** I'll see.

**SAM.** Was it good?

**ROSE.** What?

**SAM.** The gnocchi.

**ROSE.** Oh God, Sam. I don't remember, all right?

**SAM.** So, you'll see what the specials are. They usually have specials.

**ROSE.** I think I'll manage. Thanks.

*(She fusses for a while as he watches.)*

**SAM.** Do you want me to hold the pins?

**ROSE.** I'm trying to put my hair up. Why would I want you to hold the pins?

**SAM.** I meant, I could hand them to you. One at a time.

**ROSE.** No. Thanks.

*(She looks at him. He is so desperate to help. She hands him the hairpins.)*

Ok. Thanks.

**SAM.** No problemo!

*(pause)* So, Richard Miller. How about that.

**ROSE.** Mmhmm.

**SAM.** What does he do now, did you say?

**ROSE.** I don't know.

**SAM.** He didn't mention what he did? For a living?

**ROSE.** I imagine I'll find out tonight.

**SAM.** So what did you talk about?

**ROSE.** His daughter just got married. Caroline.

**SAM.** He has a daughter?

**ROSE.** Well, obviously, if she just got married. Could you hand me a pin? I mean, if you're going to hold them…

**SAM.** So, he's married.

**ROSE.** His wife died.

**SAM.** Oh. That's terrible.

**ROSE.** I mean, she didn't jump off a boat or anything.

**SAM.** Your hair looks nice like that. Up, like that. I always liked it like that.

**ROSE.** Don't you have something to do? You really don't have to stand over me while I get ready.

**SAM.** I like to watch you.

**ROSE.** Oh please.

**SAM.** What?

**ROSE.** You like to watch me.

**SAM.** I do.

**ROSE.** You like to watch me because I'm going out with another man tonight. For twenty-five years you didn't like to watch me.

**SAM.** Yeah. I don't know. I guess you're right.

**ROSE.** Yeah.

**SAM.** So stupid. It's so great to watch you. Why didn't I want to watch you?

**ROSE.** This is really exhausting, Sam. I'm very nervous. This is my first date in a long time. I don't have the energy to give you right now, okay?

**SAM.** Because you're going out on a date.

**ROSE.** That's right.

**SAM.** With another man.

**ROSE.** Yes.

**SAM.** While your husband stays home. And eats a sandwich in front of the TV. Because I will. Make a sandwich. I can make a sandwich.

**ROSE.** You could go out. Call Allyson Mendelson.

**SAM.** You don't want me to do that.

**ROSE.** Do whatever you want.

**SAM.** I don't want to do it Rose. I don't. Want to do that. Any more.

**ROSE.** It's up to you.

**SAM.** I can't really catch up with this. I don't understand. The rules. I don't…

**ROSE.** Look. I thought you were dead. What was I supposed to think? I had to move on.

**SAM.** It's only been a week.

**ROSE.** You left me.

**SAM.** I told you. I wasn't leaving you. I heard this beautiful…

**ROSE.** Yeah yeah yeah. Please don't tell me that again, okay? I was saying that I felt I couldn't live with you – with you not caring for me any more and you jumped overboard. I don't know what your version is but that's my version. You jumped overboard. Rather than even respond to me, rather than try to dissuade me, you jumped overboard. And swam away!

**SAM.** I was following…

**ROSE.** Stop! As far as I'm concerned we're…separated. You can do whatever you want.

**SAM.** Separated.

**ROSE.** Yes.

(*She considers her hair done. She puts on her top. It is loud and skimpy – the sort of thing one would find at Mandee's or another teen shop.* **SAM** *automatically zips it up in the back.*)

**SAM.** What am I supposed to do now? Do you want me to move out?

(**ROSE** *has never considered this.*)

**ROSE.** What would you eat?

**SAM.** I don't know.

**ROSE.** You've never even made the coffee.

**SAM.** I guess I could learn. If that's what you wanted.

**ROSE.** Who would do your wash?

**SAM.** I should learn how to do these things. Anyway. Right? So that you don't have to do them. Right? I mean, all the time? So that you don't have to do them all the time?

**ROSE.** Do you want to move out?

**SAM.** No!

**ROSE.** You sound like you want to move out.

**SAM.** Of course I don't.

**ROSE.** Then why don't you say that!? Why don't you put up a fight? Why don't you say, "We are not separated. We are married. You shouldn't be going out with another man and I'm not going to move out and you're going to make the coffee." Why don't you say that?

**SAM.** Is that what you want me to say?

**ROSE.** God. Forget it.

*(She puts on her skirt. It is tight and far too short. Clearly from the same shop. She looks in the mirror and takes herself in.)*

How do I look?

**SAM.** That's...that's not how you usually dress.

**ROSE.** So?

**SAM.** So...I'm just...surprised.

**ROSE.** Does it look good?

**SAM.** Yeah...where did you get it?

**ROSE.** At a store, Sam. Where am I going to get it? I wove it out of flax.

**SAM.** They look...young.

**ROSE.** So? Why shouldn't I look young?

**SAM.** No. It's good. It's good.

**ROSE.** *(putting on thigh high spiky boots)* Why shouldn't I show off what I've got? I see you staring at the girls, the girls who dress like this. So why shouldn't I wear it.

**SAM.** You look good. Richard's lucky. You look nice.

**ROSE.** Nice?

**SAM.** One piece of hair isn't up.

**ROSE.** Where?

**SAM.** In the back.

**ROSE.** Where?

**SAM.** Here.

*(He takes a pin and tries to put it up, but can't manage.)*

**ROSE.** Oh, for Christ's sake.

*(She takes the pin from him and fixes her hair.)*

OK. I guess I'm ready.

**SAM.** Don't go out with another man. You're married to me. We're not separated. You make the coffee.

**ROSE.** Don't wait up.

*(blackout)*

## Scene Six

*(**ROSE** is at a table at the restaurant waiting. She is nursing a glass of wine. The **WAITRESS**, played by the **SIREN**, approaches the table.)*

**WAITRESS.** Can I get you another?

**ROSE.** No, I'm sure he'll be here any minute.

**WAITRESS.** Yeah…Do you want to order an appetizer, and then…

**ROSE.** You asked me that. I'll wait.

**WAITRESS.** The thing is, we have a second seating at 9. So…

**ROSE.** We'll eat fast. Once he comes.

**WAITRESS.** I mean, I don't want to be rude…

**ROSE.** Oh, good! I thought you did want to be rude.

**WAITRESS.** Huh?

**ROSE.** I'm sorry. I'm kind of nervous.

**WAITRESS.** Ok. *(She starts to leave.)*

**ROSE.** Do I look…

**WAITRESS.** Yeah?

**ROSE.** How do I look?

**WAITRESS.** Well…

**ROSE.** Do I look…old?

**WAITRESS.** You look about my mother's age. Why, how old are you?

**ROSE.** Never mind.

*(The **WAITRESS** looks at her.)*

**WAITRESS.** My sister has that same outfit. In blue.

**ROSE.** Yeah? So…is it…. You like it?

**WAITRESS.** She's like sixteen.

**ROSE.** Oh God. I will take another wine. Wait.

*(She tosses back the rest of the glass and hands it to the **WAITRESS**.)*

**WAITRESS.** Will do.

(**ROSE**'s *cell phone rings. The ringtone is her song – Rose Adelle. She gropes through her bag to find it.*)

**ROSE.** See. That's probably him. I'm sure he's on his way.

**WAITRESS.** Okay.

*(She leaves. **ROSE** finds and answers her phone.)*

**ROSE.** Hello? What are you doing calling me? Well, you are interrupting. I don't know. I haven't ordered yet. He isn't here…yet. No, it's still early. Don't, all right? I'm not interested. So write it. But don't write it for me. I don't want any more songs.

*(She sees **RICHARD**. Stunned.)*

Oh my God.

*(She hangs up.)*

(**RICHARD** *enters. He is played by an actor in his early 20's. He looks great. Thin, Full head of hair. But he walks stiffly.*)

**RICHARD.** Rose?

**ROSE.** Richard.

**RICHARD.** Ciao Bella! I'm so sorry! We should have exchanged cell numbers! I couldn't reach you.

**ROSE.** Oh my God.

**RICHARD.** I threw my back out. I got this back thing. I'm really sorry. I called your house to say I'd be late and this dude answered. Said you'd already left. He sounded…

**ROSE.** You haven't…you look just the same.

**RICHARD.** You too. You look just the same. I would know you anywhere.

**ROSE.** No. But you…haven't changed at *all.*

**RICHARD.** You too.

**ROSE.** You look twenty to me.

**RICHARD.** You too.

*(She goes to hug him.)*

**ROSE.** It's so good to see you Richard. I can't get over...

**RICHARD.** Oy...Oh, careful. Sorry to be such an old fart. But when my back goes...

**ROSE.** No, I know. Here. Let me help you sit down. Here.

*(He sits, like an old man. They pause and look at each other.)*

**RICHARD.** So...you look great. La molto bella signora.

**ROSE.** Yeah? You look...unbelievably great.

**RICHARD.** You were always a hottie.

**ROSE.** A hottie?

**RICHARD.** That's what they say now. The kids. Someone they like is a hottie.

**ROSE.** Yeah. No, I know. My son is...

**RICHARD.** I remember that little pink skirt – the day we went out on that boat in Central Park.

**ROSE.** Me too! I remember that too! I was just telling Sam...

**RICHARD.** Sam?

**ROSE.** That was such a wonderful day.

**RICHARD.** You were hot. I wanted to have you right then and there.

**ROSE.** You did?

**RICHARD.** I would have taken you. Right there in that boat. In front of everyone.

**ROSE.** Really?

**RICHARD.** Oh yeah. You were wearing that little pink skirt.

**ROSE.** Yeah?

**RICHARD.** Ho voluto prendere sotto che trafora poco la gonna.

**ROSE.** That's beautiful. What does that mean?

**RICHARD.** I wanted to get under that little pink skirt.

**ROSE.** Oh.

**RICHARD.** You betcha. You were the bomb.

**ROSE.** Huh. *(beat)* You never even kissed me.

**RICHARD.** Sure I did.

**ROSE.** No. I thought…I thought you weren't that interested in me. That way. I mean, it was very romantic, but you didn't even…

**RICHARD.** Are you sure? I thought I got to second base that day.

**ROSE.** What?

**RICHARD.** I remember telling my buddy Mike. I got to second base that day.

**ROSE.** You told your friend Mike.

**RICHARD.** Sorry. Shouldn't kiss and tell.

**ROSE.** You never even kissed me. You never held my hand.

*(He reaches across the table and takes her hand.)*

**RICHARD.** I'm holding your hand now.

**ROSE.** *(very flushed)* Oh. Yes.

*(He kisses each of her fingers.)*

**RICHARD.** I kissed you this time.

*(**ROSE** sits flustered.)*

**ROSE.** So…Richard…

**RICHARD.** Rosie.

**ROSE.** Does…does your daughter live in Long Island too? Where does…

**RICHARD.** Let's talk about us.

**ROSE.** Our son, Barry…he's in school in Vermont…

*(Her cell phone rings. She hesitates, then answers it.)*

What? No, I'm fine. He's here. I'm sorry, Richard.

**RICHARD.** No. That's ok. You're a popular lady.

**ROSE.** Ok. I'm going now. I don't know yet. Look, I'm going to go. Don't. Don't sing it. I don't want to hear it. No. Ok bye. I'm hanging up! Bye. Sorry about that.

**RICHARD.** Rose. Rosie. I was sorry to hear about your loss.

**ROSE.** Yes. You too.

**RICHARD.** What was his name…I'm sorry.

**ROSE.** Sam Abrams.

**RICHARD.** Sam Abrams...

**ROSE.** You were in the same dorm. Remember?

**RICHARD.** I only remember you, Rosie. Ho avuto solo degli occhi per lei.

**ROSE.** But don't you remember when Sam asked me out and...

**RICHARD.** I was crazy about you.

**ROSE.** You were, right?

**RICHARD.** Sure.

**ROSE.** That's what I told him.

**RICHARD.** Who?

**ROSE.** And do you think...I mean, if we'd gotten together. Or...

**RICHARD.** I think there would have been fireworks.

**ROSE.** No. I mean, if we'd stayed together. If we'd...wound up together...

**RICHARD.** Well, it really hadn't gotten to that stage.

**ROSE.** Right.

**RICHARD.** You've got gorgeous eyes, Rose.

**ROSE.** Thanks. But if we had. I mean, if you hadn't left...If I hadn't gone out with Sam...

**RICHARD.** Well, I got that job.

**ROSE.** Right.

**RICHARD.** In Roma.

**ROSE.** Right. I just think about...how great we were. Together.

**RICHARD.** It was magic.

**ROSE.** Yeah? For me too. If Sam hadn't written me that song...I always thought you and I...

**RICHARD.** Yes. So...have you seen many men since your husband passed? *(pause)*

**ROSE.** Ummm, I need to tell you about that.

*(The **WAITRESS** comes over with **ROSE**'s wine.)*

**WAITRESS.** Ah...he showed up!

**RICHARD.** Hello.

**ROSE.** How old does he look to you?

**WAITRESS.** Uh…he looks about my father's age. Do you want to hear the specials, or do you know what you'd like.

**RICHARD.** *(reaching for* **ROSE***'s hand.)* I've already got something special.

**WAITRESS.** So…no then.

*(***RICHARD*** just stares at* **ROSE***.)*

See, your reservation was for seven? So…if you would like to order your dinner now…

**RICHARD.** Get me a bottle of your finest wine.

**WAITRESS.** There's a wide variety. Do you want the wine list?

**RICHARD.** Surprise me.

**WAITRESS.** Red or white?

**RICHARD.** Surprise me. I like to be surprised.

**WAITRESS.** Will do. *(She leaves.)*

**RICHARD.** Where were we?

**ROSE.** The thing is…when I called you, Sam had had this boating incident?

**RICHARD.** You said. So tragic. When was that?

**ROSE.** Yeah. That's the thing. That was last week.

**RICHARD.** Last week?

**ROSE.** I…I thought he was gone. Or…he was gone. I mean, they couldn't find him. They just thought…we all thought he was gone. Dead.

**RICHARD.** Right…

**ROSE.** And then he turned up.

**RICHARD.** His body? Wait, did he turn up last week, or he went missing last week?

**ROSE.** It all happened last week.

**RICHARD.** Interesting.

**ROSE.** And he turned up…alive. Actually. Yes.

**RICHARD.** Oh! Well…wonderful. Right?

**ROSE.** But…when I called you, I thought I was a…a widow. When actually…

**RICHARD.** So that was him on the phone? When I called your house?

**ROSE.** Yes.

**RICHARD.** I hope I didn't make things uncomfortable. I mean, was our tryst supposed to remain secret or…

**ROSE.** No! No. He knows. He knows I'm out. With you.

**RICHARD.** Oh! So, you have one of those open marriages.

**ROSE.** We're separated.

**RICHARD.** You just get more and more intriguing to me.

**ROSE.** I do?

**RICHARD.** You smell good. It's intoxicating.

**ROSE.** Thanks.

**RICHARD.** Rose. Rose Jacobs.

**ROSE.** Ummmm.

**RICHARD.** Have you dated much? Since you were…separated?

**ROSE.** It's only been…a few days.

**RICHARD.** So…No?

**ROSE.** No! Of course not.

**RICHARD.** So, I will be the first man you've been with in… how many years have you been married?

**ROSE.** How do you mean been with?

**RICHARD.** Twenty? Twenty-five?

**ROSE.** We just celebrated our twenty-fifth wedding anniversary. In fact, we were on a cruise for our twenty-fifth…

*(Her cell phone rings. She decides to ignore it.)*

**RICHARD.** What if we take our dinner to go?

**ROSE.** What? Why would we…

**RICHARD.** Do you need to get that?

**ROSE.** No. No, I don't.

*(She flips the phone open and closes it so that the ringing stops.)*

**RICHARD.** Let's tell the waitress we're going to take it to go.

**ROSE.** We just ordered wine. I don't…This is all so bizarre. Richard. I feel like…you haven't changed at all, but then you're completely…

**RICHARD.** Different? The years have mellowed me. Like a fine wine.

*(At that moment the **WAITRESS** comes back with the bottle of wine.)*

Speaking of which.

*(to the **WAITRESS**)* You must have supernatural, telepathic powers.

**WAITRESS.** Okay.

*(holding up the bottle)* I surprised you. With our most expensive bottle.

*(She pours a glass.)* Do you need to smell it and taste it or can I just pour?

*(He sloshes it around and smells it and tastes it.)*

**RICHARD.** Magnifico. We would like two orders of the fillet mignon, and we would like to have it to go. Is that possible?

**ROSE.** No. Wait.

**WAITRESS.** That would be great actually.

**ROSE.** Why don't we just eat here…

**RICHARD.** Wonderful. We'll drink this wine while we wait.

**WAITRESS.** Sounds good. Cheers.

*(She takes the menus and leaves.)*

**ROSE.** No no no! Richard. Where are we going?

**RICHARD.** Have you ever been to *Long Island*?

*(Whenever he says "Long Island" it sounds like a distant, exotic place.)*

**ROSE.** Of course I've been to Long Island. But why don't we just eat our…

**RICHARD.** You've never been to this part of *Long Island*. You're in for a special treat.

*(He raises his glass to her.)* To us.

**ROSE.** Richard, I'm not...I need some time.

**RICHARD.** You can take all the time you want.

**ROSE.** Maybe I should just go home. I'm feeling very...

**RICHARD.** You're not feeling well?

**ROSE.** ...sad.

**RICHARD.** No! No, don't feel sad. Sweetheart.

*(Her phone rings again.)*

**ROSE.** *(answering it)* Don't call me any more! That's it. Or I'm turning the phone off! I mean it. *(She hangs up.)*

**RICHARD.** Why don't you just turn it off?

**ROSE.** Well, if there's an emergency I want him to be able to...No. You're right. I'm turning it off.

*(She does.)*

**RICHARD.** Good bella. Now it's just us. Let's drink up this wine. Mmmm. It's very nice.

**ROSE.** I can't go home. Till much later. Sam can't think this didn't go well.

**RICHARD.** Isn't this going well? I think it could go very, very well.

**ROSE.** I have to come in late. He needs to worry. A fraction of the amount he made me worry. He made me sick. I thought my life was over. It's been a terrible week.

**RICHARD.** He doesn't deserve you.

**ROSE.** Maybe. Probably he does.

*(She starts crying.)* I probably deserve him.

**RICHARD.** No. Sweetheart. Don't cry. Come now. Drink your wine. We have a whole bottle to drink. And then we'll have a nice dinner on *Long Island*.

**ROSE.** Do you have a guest room? Or...your daughter's room...

**RICHARD.** Let's see how we feel. Come. To us.

*(**SAM** enters, looking around wildly. Maybe he has a guitar around his neck.)*

**SAM.** Rose!

**ROSE.** Sam. What are you doing here?

**SAM.** Rose. What the hell. Have you been crying?

**ROSE.** No.

**SAM.** Did he make you cry?

**ROSE.** I'm fine. You remember Richard? Richard, Sam.

**RICHARD.** No. I don't think so.

**SAM.** Yeah. I remember you.

**ROSE.** Isn't it amazing? How little he's changed? It's unbelievable, isn't it?

**SAM.** No. He looks…old.

**ROSE.** Really? He looks twenty to me.

**RICHARD.** And you look twenty to me, Rose.

  *(to* **SAM***)* Would you care to join us for a drink?

**SAM.** No.

**RICHARD.** Before we go?

**SAM.** Where are we going?

**RICHARD.** Rose and I. To my place. On *Long Island*.

**SAM.** No you're not.

**ROSE.** Sam. You should leave.

**SAM.** She's not going anywhere with you. She's coming home with me. Right now. I'm going to make us both…sandwiches.

**RICHARD.** We've ordered the fillet mignon.

**SAM.** She doesn't like that.

**RICHARD.** I think you're mistaken.

**SAM.** If you'd spent twenty-five years with her you'd know she likes the gnocchi here.

**RICHARD.** Well, anything you like. Anything on the menu. Or anywhere really. Anywhere in town. Or *Long Island*. I will get you whatever suits your fancy.

  *(The* **WAITRESS** *approaches with the to-go bags.)*

**WAITRESS.** Here you go. And here's the check. Thanks for coming!

  *(seeing* **SAM***)* Hi! Do you have a…reservation?

**SAM.** Come on Rose. We're going home.

**WAITRESS.** Wait. Don't I know you?

**SAM.** I don't think so. Where's your coat, sweetheart?

**WAITRESS.** Scrabulous!

**SAM.** Oh my God.

**ROSE.** Oh my God.

**WAITRESS.** We met for coffee! Remember? Sam, right? You were so funny!

**ROSE.** He's hilarious.

**SAM.** Rose.

**WAITRESS.** You never called. Do you still have my number?

**RICHARD.** You really have an interesting marriage, Rosie.

**SAM.** I'm not doing that. I'm sorry. I'm not doing that any more.

**WAITRESS.** What?

**SAM.** Scrabble…coffee. Any more. I'm…this is my wife. Rose.

**WAITRESS.** Oh.

**ROSE.** Come on, Richard.

**RICHARD.** *(pulling out his credit card and giving it to the* **WAITRESS***)* Settle us up please.

**SAM.** Rose. Listen.

**RICHARD.** I think she doesn't want to listen to you. I think she's made it clear.

**SAM.** Let me sing you the song, Rosie. Please.

**ROSE.** I've heard enough.

**SAM.** I think you'll like it. I wrote it without even trying. All that feeling. It's back. It's about you, Rose.

**RICHARD.** Why don't you record it and send it to her?

**SAM.** Why don't you step outside.

**ROSE.** What?

**RICHARD.** What?

**WAITRESS.** What?

**SAM.** I'll fight you, you bastard.

**ROSE.** Oh my God, Sam. What are you doing?

**SAM.** Get up. I'll pound you right here.

**WAITRESS.** Well, no. Not in the restaurant.

**RICHARD.** You mean boxing?

**ROSE.** He's lost his mind. Sam, please.

**RICHARD.** I have a bad back…

>   (**SAM** *sings the song here. It is not the siren's song. It is a new song. Maybe he plays the guitar and accompanies himself with it. If not, maybe he has brought a cassette recorder with a piano accompaniment that he sings to.*)

**SAM.** *(singing)*
RICHARD MILLER'S NOT THAT GREAT.

**RICHARD.** Hey!

**SAM.**
RICHARD MILLER'S NOT THAT GREAT.

**ROSE.** Sam!

**SAM.**
RICHARD MILLER IS NOT THAT GREAT

**WAITRESS.** *(taking the credit card)* I'll ring this up. I'll just include the tip to save time.

*(She hurries off.)*

**SAM.**
OH I KNOW I'M DISAPPOINTING IN MOST EVERY SINGLE WAY. AND I KNOW YOU COULD DO BETTER.
YOU REMIND ME EVERY DAY.

**RICHARD.** You can do better, Rose.

**SAM.**
BUT I REALIZE THAT THE LIFE I LIVE IS EMPTY FOR ME ROSE. IF YOU'RE NOT THERE BESIDE ME YELLING "SAM PICK UP YOUR CLOTHES."

**ROSE.** Oh my God, Sam. Not here.

**SAM.**
RICHARD MILLER'S NOT THAT GREAT

**ROSE.** I'm sorry Richard.

**SAM.**
RICHARD MILLER'S NOT THAT GREAT. RICHARD MILLER IS NOT THAT GREAT.
MY BATTERIES ARE RUNNING DOWN, AND YOURS ARE TOO I KNOW.
BUT EVEN THOUGH THE CHARGE IS DIM, YOU HAVEN'T LOST YOUR GLOW.
THERE ARE BILLIONS OF OTHER PEOPLE ON THIS LITTLE SPINNING BALL.
BUT IF YOU'RE THE ONE I DIE WITH ROSE, IT'S NOT SO BAD AT ALL.
RICHARD MILLER'S NOT THAT GREAT.
RICHARD MILLER'S NOT THAT GREAT.
RICHARD MILLER IS NOT THAT GREAT.

**SAM.** Rose. I would choose you. If we met today. Would you choose me?

**ROSE.** If we met today…probably not.

**SAM.** Oh.

**ROSE.** But twenty-five years ago I chose you, Sam. And… that's always been enough for me.

**SAM.** Thank you Rose.

**RICHARD.** Wait…Does that mean you're not coming to *Long Island?*

**ROSE.** No, Richard. I'm sorry.

**SAM.** Thank you, Rose. You won't be sorry. I'll make sure every day that you won't be sorry.

**ROSE.** Oh, Sam. I'm already sorry. But let's go home.

*(He grabs her and gives her a long passionate kiss.)*

Huh. Let's go home.

*(The **WAITRESS** returns and hands **RICHARD** back his card and the bill, which he signs.)*

**WAITRESS.** Thanks for the generous tip.

**RICHARD.** Prego, bella ragazza.

**WAITRESS.** Cool.

## Scene Seven

*(Lights shift.* **SAM** *and* **ROSE** *are on a small boat in the Mediterranean. Everything is awash with blue.)*

**SAM.** This is amazing. It's so blue.

**ROSE.** Yes.

**SAM.** And that breeze. Feels so good. Doesn't it?

**ROSE.** Mmhm.

**SAM.** I love the way the ocean smells. Particularly here. It's like perfume. There's something about…

**ROSE.** *(laughing)* You're impossible.

**SAM.** I know you think this is nuts, Rose. That I have to do this. That I have to pay her back.

**ROSE.** It is nuts.

**SAM.** But you came anyway.

**ROSE.** Of course I came.

*(a long beat)*

**SAM.** *(Taking it all in again. Filled with joy.)* My God. It's so beautiful.

**ROSE.** *(Looking all the way around her. They are in a tiny boat on a huge sea.)* Who would have thought we'd wind up here?

**SAM.** So lucky.

**ROSE.** We were Barry's age when we met. Decided to spend the next sixty, seventy years together. We were kids.

**ROSE.** It's crazy, right? We were idiots. What did we know?

**SAM.** Nothing.

**ROSE.** And nobody says – what the hell are you doing? They throw you a party.

**SAM.** Crazy.

**ROSE.** And here we are, twenty-five years later. /And we still know nothing.

**SAM.** And we still know nothing. I don't even know who I'd be if I hadn't spent my life with you. I mean, the me I am, it's from being with the you you are because you were with me.

**ROSE.** Ok…

**SAM.** Ah! This is the place. You got the package?

**ROSE.** *(sigh)* Sure. Let me tie you to the mast.

**SAM.** I really don't think you need to, Rosie. I won't jump ship again.

**ROSE.** That's great, hon. Now go stand against the mast.

**SAM.** OK.

**ROSE.** Here. Hold this.

*(She takes her knitting which is now absurdly long and wraps it around SAM.)*

**SAM.** Good. Now get the batteries.

*(She gets a large package covered in bubble wrap and plastic.)*

**ROSE.** This is hilarious.

**SAM.** Yeah.

*(Distantly at first and then louder and louder, we hear the beautiful and now heartbreakingly sad song of the SIREN. It is a wail. Long and plaintive and aching. Only SAM can hear it.)*

**ROSE.** You hear it.

**SAM.** Throw it in, honey.

*(She hurls the package overboard. We hear a splash. They both stand watching it float away for a moment.)*

*(And then the Siren's song goes from its mournful minor key, back to its original lovely melody. SAM is filled with feeling. He reaches for ROSE.)*

**ROSE.** What does it sound like?

**SAM.** *(filled with emotion)* It sounds like…you.

*(She goes to him. He wraps the remaining scarf around her and they stand together..)*

**ROSE.** She's going to need more batteries.

**SAM.** We'll have to come back. Every five years.

**ROSE.** No. Every year.

*(They kiss.)*

**SAM.** I choose you, Rose Adelle Abrams.
**ROSE.** Yeah. Crazy. I choose you, too.

*(They stand, tied together as the lights swell to brilliant color, the music swells and then)*

*(blackout)*

**End of Play**

# See what people are saying about
# SIRENS...

"The breakout hit of this Humana Festival is sure to be *Sirens*. Deborah Zoe Laufer has tackled — with great humor and some genuine poignancy — a sensitive subject painfully familiar to many couples: a marriage that has lost its spark...Suffice it to say Laufer has written some of the most delectable and amusing dialogue we've heard on a stage in a long time. *Sirens* feels fresh, smart and hugely entertaining."
– *Chicago Sun-Times*

"Laufer's funny and heartfelt *Sirens*...proving that character and story — not to mention romance — are alive and well in American theater. *Sirens* is a witty play with a heart as big as its mouth."
– *Louisville Courier-Journal*

"The Festival's smash this year was Ms. Laufer's *Sirens*...Ms. Laufer has a wonderful theatrical imagination and a fine comic sense."
– *TheatreMania.com*

Also by
# Deborah Zoe Laufer...

# End Days

# The Last Schwartz

# Out of Sterno

Please visit our website **samuelfrench.com** for complete descriptions and licensing information.

# OTHER TITLES AVAILABLE FROM SAMUEL FRENCH

## END DAYS

Deborah Zoe Laufer

*Comedy / 3m, 2f / Interior*

Sixteen year-old Rachel Stein is having a bad year. Her father hasn't changed out of his pajamas since 9/11. Her mother has begun a close, personal relationship with Jesus. Her new neighbor, a sixteen year-old Elvis impersonator, has fallen for her hard. And the Apocalypse is coming Wednesday. Her only hope is that Stephen Hawking will save them all.

**End Days received the 2008 American Theatre Critics Association Steinberg citation.**

"The universality of the denouement brings this comedy full circle, leaving us to admire the relevancy of Laufer's humor and wisdom of her message."
– *Variety*

"Rapturously funny play about a family trying to survive in a world hurtling toward Armageddon, proves that the right playwright can inspire healing laughter in even the most sobering subjects."
– *The Miami Herald*

"Both poignantly redemptive and often hilariously funny. I hope others will have the opportunity to see this special play. It begs the question of what we would hold most sacred if we knew the end was near. And it brings to life our broad range of choices, including laughter, and the treasured traveling companions who are there even when we face our own personal Armageddon."
– *Huffington Post*

"*End Days* may be about a weirdly dysfunctional family that finds its soul by waiting for the Apocalypse together, but this play has heart: It's engaging, funny as hell and even touching...An exceptional show"
– *NUVO* (Indianapolis)

SAMUELFRENCH.COM

# OTHER TITLES AVAILABLE FROM SAMUEL FRENCH

## THE LAST SCHWARTZ

### Deborah Zoe Laufer

*Comedy / 3m, 3f / Interior*

The Schwartz family is on its last legs. Their father's dead and their Catskills home is up for sale. Norma's husband hasn't spoken to her since she turned their 15 year old son in for smoking pot. After five miscarriages it appears Herb's wife won't provide him with an heir. Simon has one foot on the moon. Gene's girlfriend is about to have an abortion. And nobody seems very clear about what it is to be a family anyway.

What is it to be a family? Does anybody care any more? Is Judaism all there is to hold the family together? Or is that what it will take to push the family apart? As Simon says, the Earth as we know it is really on its last legs too. When all of mankind is blown into oblivion, who's going to care whether there were Jews? Or how hard a few generations fought to keep the faith alive?

*The Cherry Orchard* takes a holiday in the Catskills as the Schwartz family congregates, maybe for the last time, on the one-year anniversary of their father's death.

"incendiary drama and wickedly self-deprecating humor...she shows herself to be a vital new voice for the theater willing to wade into potentially abrasive waters and skillful enough to cut the sting with laughter."
– *Palm Beach Post*

"A beautifully crafted new play that weaves hilarity, mystery and loss into a resonant tale about a family's disintegration."
– *The Miami Herald*

"*The Last Schwartz* is rollicking, sad, shocking, goofy, and thoughtful. It is comic drama firing on all cylinders, a superb work of theater by a playwright in full command of her considerable gift for character and dialogue."
– *The Washington Times*

SAMUELFRENCH.COM

# OTHER TITLES AVAILABLE FROM SAMUEL FRENCH

## OUT OF STERNO

Deborah Zoe Laufer

*Comedy / 2m, 2f / Multiple Sets*

Dotty's life in Sterno with her husband Hamel is absolutely perfect! It's a fairy tale, it really is. True, in their seven years of marriage Hamel has forbidden her to leave their tiny apartment or speak to anyone, but Dotty is so very happy to spend her days watching video re-enactments of the day they first met. When a phone call from a mysterious woman threatens to tear her world asunder, Dotty must venture out into the vast city of Sterno, and try to discover what it is to be a "real" woman.

*Out of Sterno* is a coming-of-age play in an *Alice in Wonderland* world. It explores the triumph and heartbreak of growing up and the contradictory societal pressures women face just trying to make it across town.

SAMUELFRENCH.COM

# OTHER TITLES AVAILABLE FROM SAMUEL FRENCH

## FUENTE

Cusi Cram

*Dramatic Comedy /4m, 2f / Multiple Sets*

Something is not right. There is a secret humidity in the air in a town where the breezes have been on strike for two hundred years. Soledad thinks she is Alexis Carrington from Dynasty and feels itchy. Chaparro can't seem to scratch her itch anymore. Esteban might just be the man for the job. And Adela watches it all unfold as if it were a soap opera on TV. Maybe it is? Anything is possible in Fuente, an almost-real town, somewhere between where North America ends and South America begins.

*Fuente* is a magically-real comedy set in a remote desert town about love, revenge, escape, and the perilous powers of Aqua Net hairspray.

"The play, *Fuente*, is powerful, moving and original, which after a three-year development process and a Herrick Theatre Foundation Prize for New Play, is being given a smartly staged, well acted world premiere at Boyd's smaller venue in Sheffield. Cram has written a small-scale at once real and mythical epic about love, vengeance and one's sense of place. The language is earthy (this is NOT a family show!) and poetic. The characters and their stories are sad but also funny enough to have the audience burst out laughing. The Garcia Marquez-like magic is amusingly propelled by a bottle of Aqua Net hair spray."
– *CurtainUp.com*

www.ingramcontent.com/pod-product-compliance
Lightning Source LLC
Chambersburg PA
CBHW070649300426
44111CB00013B/2340